© 1999 Havoc Publishing
Artwork © 1999 Diane Arthurs
Under license from Penny Lane Publishing, Inc.

ISBN 1-57977-156-4

Published by Havoc Publishing
San Diego, California

Made in China

www.havocpub.com

Havoc Publishing
9808 Waples Street
San Diego, California 92121

This Record Book Celebrates

_____

and

_____

Contents

Contents

Mom, when you were young...

Mom, tell me a little about yourself when you were growing up _____

_____

_____

_____

Where did you live? _____

Tell me who some of your friends were _____

Mom, where did you go to high school? _____

What are some of your favorite memories from that period of your life?

_____

_____

Tell me about what you did after high school _____

_____

_____

_____

Mom, tell me about where and when you first met Dad. What were your first thoughts and impressions of him?_____

_____

_____

How long did you and Dad date before you got engaged?_____
How did Dad propose?_____

_____

What was your wedding like? Tell me a little about the ceremony _____

_____

_____

When did you first find out you were pregnant with me? _____

_____

Tell me about being pregnant. What were some of your thoughts and feelings?

_____

_____

_____

_____

_____

Daughter, when you were young...

Daughter, let me tell you about the day you were born _____

_____

_____

_____

Did I tell you how we chose your name? _____

_____

Did I tell you how I felt the first time that I held you in my arms?

_____

_____

Do you remember our first house? _____

_____

_____

Tell me what you remember about your bedroom growing up

_____
_____
_____

List here some of your favorite neighborhood playmates _____

_____
_____

Do you remember playing games, riding bikes and playing sports?

_____
_____
_____

Do you remember our family pets? _____

_____
_____
_____

Daughter, when you were little we would spend a lot of time together. Tell me some of your favorite memories about being Mommy's little girl _____

_____

_____

_____

_____

Tell me about some of your favorite things to play with when you were little. Do you remember your favorite schoolmates? _____

_____

_____

_____

_____

Tell me, Mom, about the schools that I went to. How did you pick them? Were they close by? _____

_____

_____

Remembering back, I liked these teachers and subjects the best. _____

_____

_____

_____

Daughter, I can remember you making such thoughtful gifts for me in school. Some of my favorites are the following. Do remember these? _____

_____

_____

_____

_____

_____

_____

_____

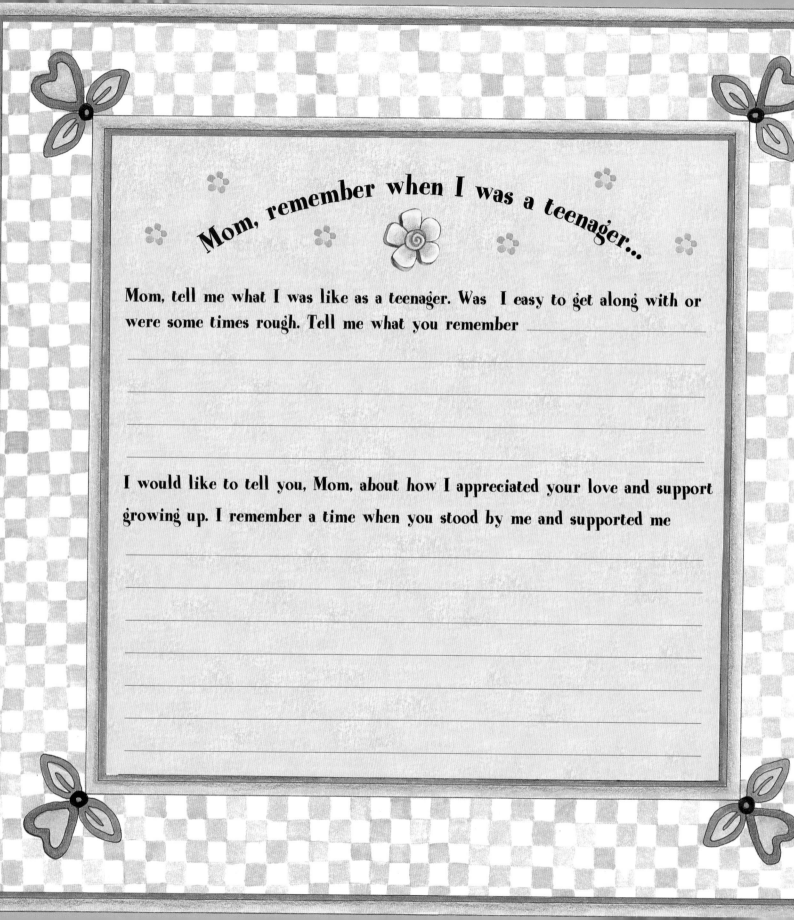

Mom, remember when I was a teenager...

Mom, tell me what I was like as a teenager. Was I easy to get along with or were some times rough. Tell me what you remember _____

_____

_____

_____

I would like to tell you, Mom, about how I appreciated your love and support growing up. I remember a time when you stood by me and supported me

_____

_____

_____

_____

_____

_____

_____

Tell me about our family...

Mom, tell me one of your favorite stories about our family. What were we doing together? How old were we? _____

_____

_____

_____

_____

_____

_____

_____

_____

_____

_____

_____

©Diane Arthurs

Family Photograph

Family Photograph

Some of my favorite stories...

Mom, do you know that some my fondest childhood memories are about spending time with you? I would like to tell you about some of my favorite stories.

_____

_____

_____

_____

_____

_____

_____

_____

_____

_____

_____

_____

_____

_____

_____

Like Mother, Like Daughter...

Mom, we are alike in so many ways. These are some of your characteristics that I have inherited _____

_____

_____

_____

_____

I notice these qualities about my personality that I know come from you

_____

_____

_____

Tell me, Mom, why you think we are so alike _____

_____

_____

_____

My darling daughter, I would love to tell you about all of the great things that I see in you. I feel that these are some of your best qualities _____

_____

_____

_____

Do you know that I am proud to see some of my qualities in you? I am so

proud that you inherited this from me _____

_____

_____

_____

I would like to tell you that I have also inherited something from you. This is

a quality about myself that you have helped me to develop _____

_____

_____

_____

We are alike, you and me...

Mom, I enjoy the fact that we share similar interests. Do you know that I am happiest that we share these hobbies? _____

_____

_____

_____

_____

Tell me, Mom, about your favorite things that we share. What are the things we

have in common that you enjoy most? _____

_____

_____

_____

_____

_____

_____

_____

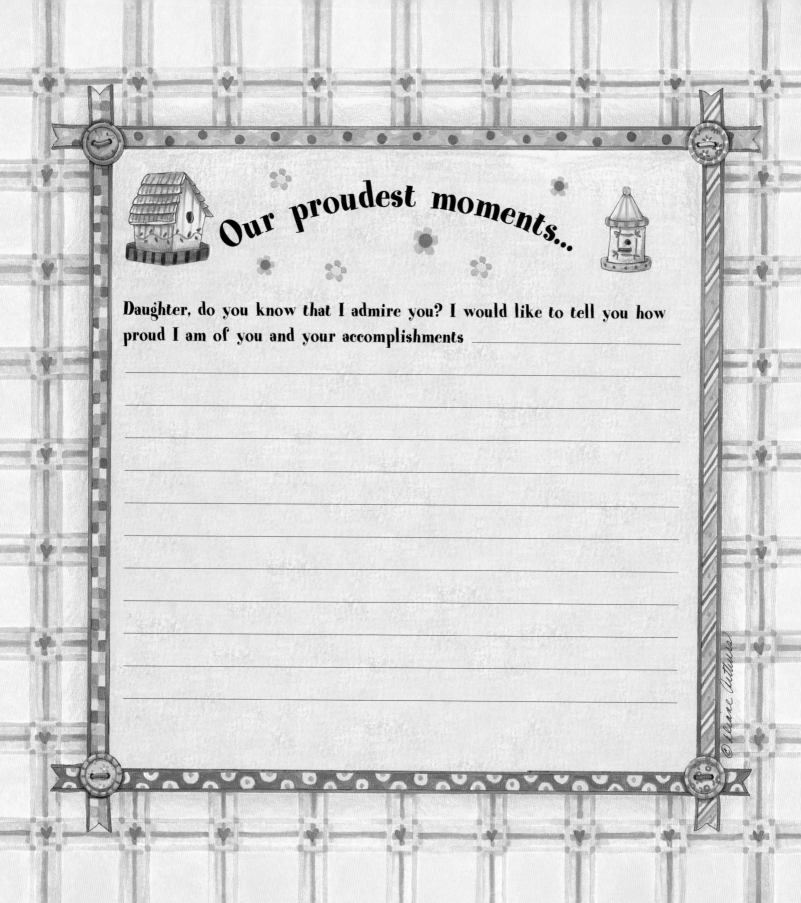

Our proudest moments...

Daughter, do you know that I admire you? I would like to tell you how proud I am of you and your accomplishments _____

_____

_____

_____

_____

_____

_____

_____

_____

_____

_____

Mom, do you know that I am proud to be your daughter? I would like to tell you about how proud I am of you and your accomplishments _____

I have learned so much from you...

Mom, you have taught me so much. A few important things I have learned that you taught me are _____

_____

_____

_____

_____

As your mother, I am glad to have helped shape you into the woman you are today. You have also taught me a few things along the way. The greatest thing that you have taught me is _____

_____

_____

_____

_____

_____

_____

Do you remember, Mom, when you warned me about something but I had to learn it the hard way? _____

_____

_____

_____

_____

_____

The greatest thing that we have learned together is _____

_____

_____

_____

_____

_____

_____

_____

_____

_____

_____

When we spend the day together...

Mom, if we could spend the whole day doing fun things together, what would you like to do? _____

_____

_____

_____

_____

I would love to spend the whole day doing this with you _____

_____

_____

_____

_____

_____

A few of our favorite things...

Mom, make a list of your favorite things. Remember to include things like movies, books, songs and foods!

_____   _____

_____   _____

_____   _____

_____   _____

_____   _____

_____   _____

_____   _____

_____   _____

_____   _____

Daughter, now it is your turn to write down your favorites. I am interested to see our similarities and differences.

_____ _____

_____ _____

_____ _____

_____ _____

_____ _____

_____ _____

_____ _____

_____ _____

_____ _____

We are fashion fanatics...

Mom, tell me how you would describe my sense of style. What are your favorite things that I wear?

_____

_____

_____

_____

_____

Mom, I would describe your style like this. My favorite places to shop with you are

_____

_____

_____

_____

_____

When we go outside...

Daughter, I love to spend quality time with you. I enjoy it when we can spend time doing these activities and hobbies together _____

_____

_____

_____

_____

_____

Mom, when it is a nice day outside I love to do these outdoor activities with you

_____

_____

_____

Tell me what your favorite outdoor activities are _____

_____

_____

When we feel like getting some exercise, I think it is great that we can do this
together _____

_____

_____

Mom, to stay healthy, what do you do? What works the best for you? _____

_____

_____

_____

Let me tell you how I stay healthy. This is what works best for me. Maybe we can
share ideas _____

_____

_____

_____

Photographs

Photographs

If I could take you away...

Mom, if you and I could take a vacation today, where would you like to go?

_____

_____

_____

_____

_____

Daughter, if I could take you away today where would you like to go?

_____

_____

_____

_____

_____

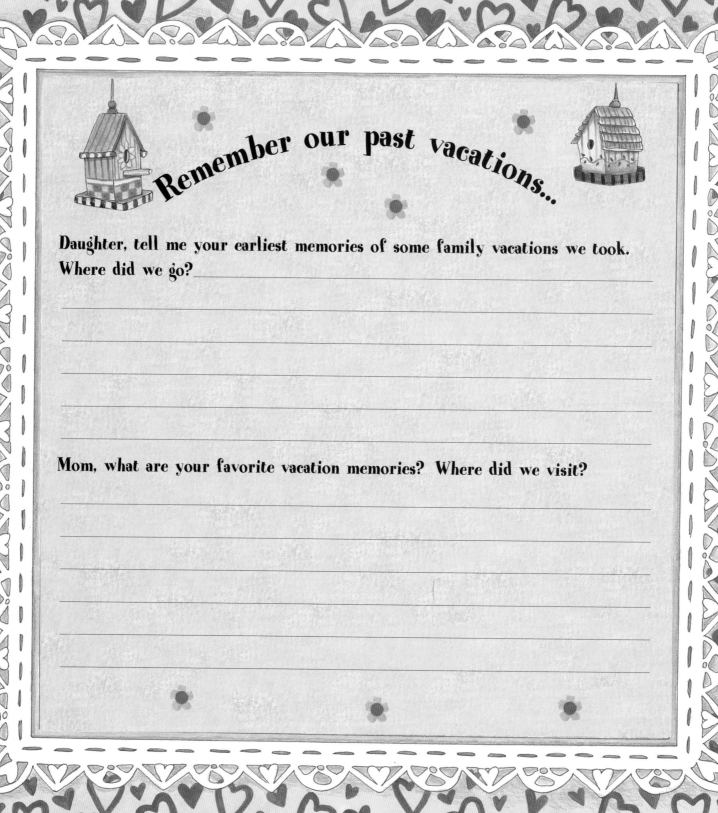

Remember our past vacations...

Daughter, tell me your earliest memories of some family vacations we took. Where did we go? _____

_____

_____

_____

_____

Mom, what are your favorite vacation memories? Where did we visit?

_____

_____

_____

_____

_____

Mom when was the first time that I went on a roller coaster? Who went with me? Was I scared? _____

_____

_____

_____

_____

_____

Did we ever go camping? Tell me, Mom, where did we go? Who went with us?

_____

_____

_____

_____

_____

_____

_____

_____

_____

_____

Attach some vacation memorabilia here

Don't forget old tickets, brochures, and maps!

Vacation Photographs

Vacation Photographs

Filling our lives with tradition...

Mom, thank you for filling my life with traditions throughout all of these years. Looking back, I can see that my life has been enriched by these special memories _____

_____

_____

_____

_____

_____

_____

_____

_____

_____

_____

_____

Daughter, I am glad that you have enjoyed that important part of our family life. One of my favorite traditions that we have is this one _____

_____

_____

_____

_____

_____

_____

_____

_____

_____

_____

_____

_____

_____

_____

_____

_____

_____

_____

_____

Bringing the family together...

Thank you, Mom, for all of the great meals that you have prepared for me. What was it like to have us all together for dinner? _____

_____

_____

_____

When I was little, what were my favorite things to eat? _____

_____

_____

Did I ever try to cook for you? How did I do? _____

_____

_____

_____

_____

_____

_____

Moms
Kitchen

Cookies

Kindness is the honey of Life
it Sweetens the cup to
the very last drop

Some spring memories...

Daughter, I can remember when you were little and we celebrated these holidays in the springtime each year _____

_____

_____

_____

_____

_____

Remembering back, you were so excited to celebrate this holiday in particular_____

_____

_____

_____

_____

_____

Fun in the summer sun...

Mom, I can remember how happy we were for summer. Tell me about some fun things that we did _____

_____

_____

_____

Where and when did I learn to swim? Who taught me? _____

_____

Mom what did you like to do during the summer? Tell me about some of the fun things that you enjoyed about summertime _____

_____

_____

_____

_____

_____

Our memories of fall...

Daughter, do you remember when we would celebrate Thanksgiving together? Thinking back, my favorite memory about Thanksgiving is _____

_____

_____

_____

_____

Mom, tell me about other holidays and celebrations in the fall. Did we celebrate Halloween? Did you ever make me a costume? _____

_____

_____

_____

_____

Memories OF Love and Laughter

Wintertime memories...

Mom, tell me about holidays that we celebrated in the winter.

_____

_____

_____

_____

_____

_____

Did I make you cards or other holiday related projects in school?

_____

_____

_____

_____

_____

_____

©Diane Arthurs

Did it ever snow at our house? Or did we ever make a special trip to the snow? Tell me about that _____

_____

_____

_____

_____

Mom, what are your favorite memories about winter holidays? Did we do special things together? _____

_____

_____

_____

_____

©Diane Arthurs

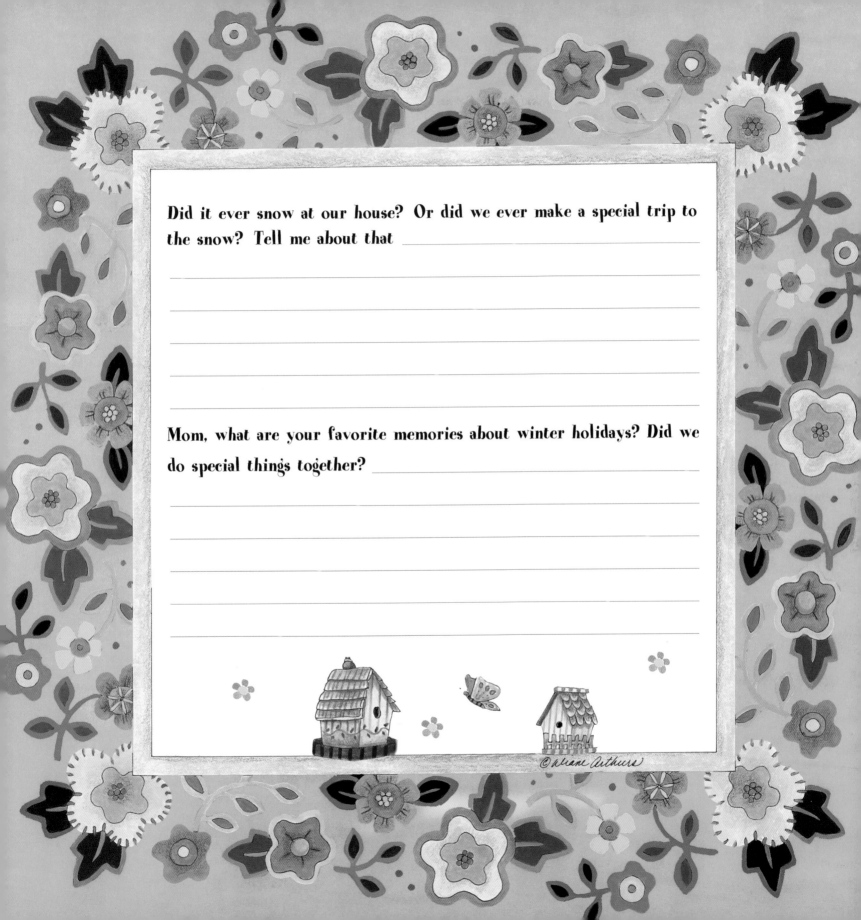

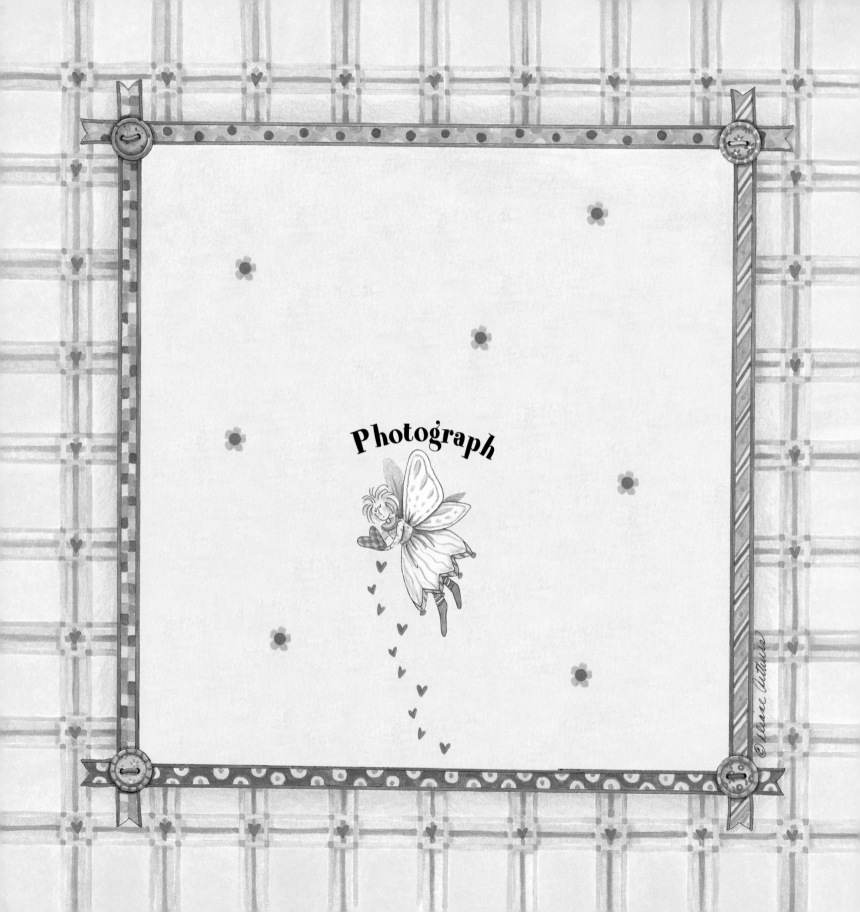

Photograph

Photograph

Our future goals together...

Daughter, let's both write down some goals we want to strive for. Tell me some of your short term goals _____

_____

_____

_____

_____

Now tell me about some of the goals that you would like to reach in the future

_____

_____

_____

_____

_____

_____

Mom, tell me some of your short term goals. When would you like to reach them?

_____

_____

_____

_____

_____

What would be some of your future goals. Tell me and I will write them down

_____

_____

_____

_____

_____

_____

_____

_____